Abraham Lincoln, Frederick Webster Osborn

American patriotic selections : famous state papers of

Washington, Jefferson, and Lincoln : with historical

introductions and critical notices

Abraham Lincoln, Frederick Webster Osborn

American patriotic selections : famous state papers of Washington, Jefferson, and Lincoln : with historical introductions and critical notices

ISBN/EAN: 9783337306342

Printed in Europe, USA, Canada, Australia, Japan

Cover: Foto ©ninafisch / pixelio.de

More available books at **www.hansebooks.com**

ENGLISH CLASSIC SERIES—No. 78.

American Patriotic Selections.

Famous State Papers

of

Washington, Jefferson, and Lincoln.

THE DECLARATION OF INDEPENDENCE.
WASHINGTON'S FAREWELL ADDRESS.
LINCOLN'S FIRST INAUGURAL.

LINCOLN'S EMANCIPATION PROCLA-
MATION.
LINCOLN'S GETTYSBURG ADDRESS.

With Historical Introductions and Critical Notices

By Frederick W. Osborn,

PROFESSOR OF MENTAL, MORAL, AND POLITICAL SCIENCE, ADELPHI ACADEMY,
BROOKLYN, N. Y.

NEW YORK:
Effingham Maynard & Co., Publishers,
771 Broadway and 67 & 69 Ninth Street,
1890.

A COMPLETE COURSE IN THE STUDY OF ENGLISH.

Spelling, Language, Grammar, Composition, Literature.

Reed's Word Lessons—A Complete Speller.
Reed & Kellogg's Graded Lessons in English.
Reed & Kellogg's Higher Lessons in English.
Kellogg's Text-Book on Rhetoric.
Kellogg's Text-Book on English Literature.

In the preparation of this series the authors have had one object clearly in view—to so develop the study of the English language as to present a complete, progressive course, from the Spelling-Book to the study of English Literature. The troublesome contradictions which arise in using books arranged by different authors on these subjects, and which require much time for explanation in the school-room, will be avoided by the use of the above "Complete Course."

Teachers are earnestly invited to examine these books.

EFFINGHAM MAYNARD & Co., Publishers,

771 Broadway, New York.

DECLARATION OF INDEPENDENCE.

INTRODUCTION.

THE first battle in the war for independence had taken place in April 1775. Since that time the colonies of New York, Massachusetts and North Carolina had been invaded by considerable armies. The king of Great Britain had issued a proclamation calling for volunteers to put down the rebellion, and had succeeded in hiring twenty thousand German troops to fight against his American subjects. Notwithstanding this state of affairs the colonies were not all agreed as to the wisdom of breaking with the mother country. Two of the leading colonies, however, Massachusetts and Virginia, were strongly in favor of such action. Accordingly on the 7th of June, Richard Henry Lee of Virginia introduced into Congress the following resolution:—"That these United Colonies are, and of right ought to be, free and independent States, that they are absolved from all allegiance to the British Crown and that all political connection between them and the State of Great Britain is and ought to be totally dissolved." —A committee of five consisting of Franklin, Sherman, Livingston, John Adams and Jefferson, were appointed to draw up such a declaration and present it to Congress. The committee unanimously agreed to leave the draft of the document to Jefferson. He submitted it to Adams and Franklin separately, for their inspection and correction, but they made but few changes in it and these were verbal. It was presented to Congress on the 2d of July, by which body it was thoroughly discussed, and some important changes were made. In particular, a passage was stricken out in which Jefferson denounced George III. for encouraging the slave-trade, and also another in which the English people are described as "unfeeling brethren." "We must endeavor to forget our former love for them and hold them as we hold the rest of mankind, enemies in war, in peace friends."

3

It was generally agreed that it would be wise to make no reflections upon the attitude of the English people. At length on July 4th, after a famous debate in which John Adams favored and John Dickinson of Pennsylvania opposed the adoption, the Declaration was adopted, all the States voting for it except New York, this State adding its approval five days later.

As a political fact the adoption of the Declaration is a landmark in our history. It marks the beginning of the history of the United States as a nation. For the first time the people of the colonies through their representatives in Congress declare themselves a distinct and separate political body. They assume the rights and powers which nations alone assume to exercise and upon the continued maintenance of which their political existence must depend. A series of causes had for many years been leading up to this event, and it is impossible to exaggerate its influence upon our subsequent political history.

THOMAS JEFFERSON.

Thomas Jefferson, the author of the Declaration of Independence, was born in Albemarle County, Va., April 2, 1743, and died at Monticello, July 4, 1826. He was one of the most distinguished statesmen of his time and his sentiments and political policy have left a permanent influence upon our institutions and government.

He was graduated at the age of nineteen from the college of William and Mary. At the age of twenty-six he was chosen to represent his county in the legislature of Virginia, and at once took an active part with those who were disposed to resist the encroachments of parliament. Between 1773 and 1775 he had written several bold and forcible state papers—one entitled, "A Summary View of the Rights of British Americans"; another, "A Reply to Lord North's Conciliatory Proposition,"—which had already established his reputation as an able advocate of constitutional freedom, and as an accomplished writer. The authorship of the Declaration added greatly to his fame both at home and abroad.

From 1776 to 1779 he was actively engaged as a member of the legislature, in accomplishing important reforms in his own State, and in 1779 he was elected Governor. After the ratification of the treaty of peace with Great Britain, in 1783, it became desirable to negotiate commercial treaties with foreign nations, and Jefferson was appointed minister to Europe for that purpose in company with Franklin and John Adams. Franklin having resigned as minister to France in 1785, Jefferson was appointed to succeed him. He was absent from the country during the formation of the Constitution, and it is well known that that document did not altogether meet his approval. Soon after his return to this country in 1789, he was offered the position of secretary of state in the cabinet of Washington. Notwithstanding his desire to return to France he concluded to accept it. In this position he became the recognized leader of the party opposed to a strong government as represented by Hamilton. After retaining this office somewhat more than four years he resigned and retired to Monticello.

In 1796, he was elected vice-president, and in 1800 president of the United States. His accession to office marked the first great victory of a new political party. His first administration was made popular by a studied simplicity in manner and in the administration of the government. The fortunate acquisition of the territory of Louisiana from France increased his popularity. A series of complications with England embarrassed his second administration and the passage of the Embargo Act beclouded its close. He withdrew from all active political life in 1809 and retired to his delightful retreat at Monticello. Here his time was employed in various literary and agricultural pursuits, and in conducting an extensive correspondence. The striking coincidence of his death with that of John Adams on the fourth of July, 1826, produced a profound impression.

He was an original thinker in politics, essentially a reformer, and was the best representative of advanced democratic ideas in government.

CRITICAL OPINIONS.

"To have been the instrument of expressing in one brief, decisive act the concentrated will and resolution of a whole family of States, . . . to have been permitted to give the impress and peculiarity of his own mind to a charter of public right destined . . . to an importance in the estimation of men equal to anything human ever borne on parchment, or expressed in the visible signs of thought—this is the glory of Thomas Jefferson."—*Eulogy of Edward Everett on Adams and Jefferson.*

"To say that he performed his great work well would be doing him injustice. To say that he did it excellently well, admirably well, would be inadequate and halting praise. Let us rather say that he so discharged the duty assigned him that all Americans may well rejoice that the work of drawing the title deed of their liberties devolved upon him."—*Webster's Works,* Vol. I., 127.

Herein lay his deep wisdom; he enjoyed a political vision, penetrating deeper down into the inevitable movement of popular government and further forward into the future trend of free institutions than was possessed by any other man in public life in his day.—*Morse's Life of Jefferson, p. 129.*

ANALYSIS OF THE DECLARATION.

A BRIEF inspection reveals the fact that the Declaration is made up of three parts. (1) The first part presents the general reasons on the part of the colonies for renouncing their allegiance to Great Britain. It asserts certain views as to the rights of man which were at that time by no means generally accepted. These were, that all men are possessed of certain natural rights which it should be the object of those intrusted with power to protect—that to the people belongs the right to establish or change a government—that when a form of government has become despotic it is the right and duty of the people to make such radical changes as may seem most likely to remove abuses and preserve their rights.

(2) The second part contains an enumeration of the tyrannical acts of the King of England, some of which were:—depriving the people of their lawful rights as English subjects, imposing taxes without their consent and cutting off their trade with other countries, sending armies of foreign soldiers among them whom they were compelled to support, and the actual waging of war and destroying the lives of the people.

(3) The third part contains the Declaration proper, in which the people of the colonies formally renounce their allegiance to Great Britain and assert their intention to exercise the political rights of free and independent States.

By the specific enumeration of the "Facts submitted to the World" it was intended to fasten upon the king rather than upon the people, the responsibility for the tyranny of which they complained. The refusal to disavow these acts, however, was deemed a sufficient reason for assuming a hostile attitude toward both the government and the people.

The original draft of this document is preserved in the Department of State at Washington. The original copy signed at Philadelphia, is to be found in the Patent Office. The bold and familiar signature of John Hancock, then President of the Congress, stands by itself and heads the list of signers.

The other names are grouped together by States, and the States are arranged in geographical order.

"It will be a memorable epoch in the history of America. It ought to be commemorated as the day of deliverance by solemn acts of devotion to Almighty God."—*John Adams.*

"The Declaration ought to be hung up in the nursery of every king, and blazoned on the porch of every palace."—*Buckle's History of Civilization in England.*

"It includes far more than it expresses; for by recognizing human equality, brotherhood and the individual as the unit of society it accepts the Christian idea of man as the basis of political institution."—*Frothingham's Rise of the Republic.*

"The Declaration had an immense effect. . . . The cause was so noble and the effort was so grand that there was not a doubt, not a hesitation in the sentiments of the entire world that governments and the rulers of States would seek glory by thinking like the people."—*Sismondi, History of the French.*

REFERENCES.—The student should consult some of the numerous biographies of Jefferson. Among the best are Randall's, Tucker's, and that of J. T. Morse in the *American Statesmen Series.* Of special interest is Jefferson's own account of the circumstances connected with the writing of the Declaration, to be found in Vol. I. of his Writings, containing his autobiography.

THE DECLARATION OF INDEPENDENCE.

In Congress, July 4, 1776.

THE UNANIMOUS DECLARATION OF THE THIRTEEN UNITED STATES OF AMERICA.

WHEN in the Course of human events, it becomes necessary for one people to dissolve the political bands which have connected them with another, and to assume among the Powers of the earth, the separate and equal station to which the Laws of Nature and of Nature's God entitle them, a decent respect to the opinions of mankind requires that they should declare the causes which impel them to the separation.

We hold these truths to be self-evident, that all men are created equal, that they are endowed by their Creator with certain unalienable Rights, that among these are Life, Liberty, and the pursuit of Happiness. That to secure these rights, Governments are instituted among Men, deriving their just powers from the consent of the governed. That whenever any Form of Government becomes destructive of these ends, it is the Right of the People to alter or to abolish it, and to institute new Government, laying its foundation on such principles and organizing its powers in such form, as to them shall seem most likely to effect their Safety and Happiness. Prudence, indeed, will dictate that Governments long established should not be changed for light and transient causes; and accordingly all experience hath shown, that mankind are more disposed to suffer, while evils are sufferable, than to right themselves by abolishing the forms to which they are accustomed. But when a long train of abuses and usurpations, pursuing invariably the same Object evinces a design to reduce them under absolute Despotism, it is their right, it is their duty, to throw off such Government, and to provide new Guards for their future security.—Such has been the patient sufferance of these Colonies; and such is now the necessity which constrains them to alter their former Systems of Government. The history of the present King of Great Britain is a history of repeated injuries and usurpations, all having in direct object the establishment of an absolute Tyranny over these States. To prove this, let Facts be submitted to a candid world.

He has refused his Assent to Laws, the most wholesome and necessary for the public good.

He has forbidden his Governors to pass Laws of immediate and pressing importance, unless suspended in their operation till his Assent should be obtained; and when so suspended, he has utterly neglected to attend to them.

He has refused to pass other Laws for the accommodation of large districts of people, unless those people would relinquish the right of Representation in the Legislature, a right inestimable to them and formidable to tyrants only.

He has called together legislative bodies at places unusual, uncomfortable, and distant from the depository of their Public Records, for the sole purpose of fatiguing them into compliance with his measures.

He has dissolved Representative Houses repeatedly, for opposing with manly firmness his invasions on the rights of the people.

He has refused for a long time, after such dissolutions, to cause others to be elected; whereby the Legislative Powers, incapable of Annihilation, have returned to the People at large for their exercise; the State remaining in the meantime exposed to all the dangers of invasion from without, and convulsions within.

He has endeavored to prevent the population of these States; for that purpose obstructing the Laws for Naturalization of Foreigners; refusing to pass others to encourage their migration hither, and raising the conditions of new Appropriations of Lands.

He has obstructed the Administration of Justice, by refusing his Assent to Laws for establishing Judiciary Powers.

He has made Judges dependent on his Will alone, for the tenure of their offices, and the amount and payment of their salaries.

He has erected a multitude of New Offices, and sent hither swarms of Officers to harass our People, and eat out their substance.

He has kept among us, in times of peace, Standing Armies without the Consent of our legislature.

He has affected to render the Military independent of and superior to the Civil Power.

He has combined with others to subject us to a jurisdiction foreign to our constitution, and unacknowledged by our laws; giving his Assent to their Acts of pretended Legislation:

For quartering large bodies of armed troops among us:

For protecting them, by a mock Trial, from Punishment for any Murders which they should commit on the Inhabitants of these States:

For cutting off our Trade with all parts of the world:

For imposing taxes on us without our Consent:

For depriving us in many cases, of the benefits of Trial by Jury:

For transporting us beyond Seas to be tried for pretended offenses:

For abolishing the free System of English Laws in a neighboring Province, establishing therein an Arbitrary government, and enlarging its Boundaries so as to render it at once an example and fit instrument for introducing the same absolute rule into these Colonies:

For taking away our Charters, abolishing our most valuable Laws, and altering fundamentally the Forms of our Governments:

For suspending our own Legislatures, and declaring themselves invested with Power to legislate for us in all cases whatsoever.

He has abdicated Government here, by declaring us out of his Protection and waging War against us.

He has plundered our seas, ravaged our Coasts, burned our towns, and destroyed the lives of our people.

He is at this time transporting large armies of foreign mercenaries to compleat the works of death, desolation, and tyranny, already begun with circumstances of Cruelty and perfidy scarcely paralleled in the most barbarous ages, and totally unworthy the Head of a civilized nation.

He has constrained our fellow Citizens taken Captive on the high Seas to bear Arms against their Country, to become the executioners of their friends and Brethren, or to fall themselves by their Hands.

He has excited domestic insurrections amongst us, and has endeavored to bring on the inhabitants of our frontiers, the merciless Indian Savages, whose known rule of warfare is an undistinguished destruction of all ages, sexes, and conditions.

In every stage of these Oppressions We have Petitioned for Redress in the most humble terms: Our repeated Petitions have been answered only by repeated injury. A Prince, whose character is thus marked by every act which may define a Tyrant, is unfit to be the ruler of a free People.

Nor have We been wanting in attention to our British brethren. We have warned them from time to time of attempts by their legislature to extend an unwarrantable jurisdiction over us. We have reminded them of the circumstances of our emigration and settlement here. We have appealed to their native justice and magnanimity, and we have conjured them by the ties of our common kindred to disavow these usurpations, which would inevitably interrupt our connections and correspondence. They too have been deaf to the voice of justice and of consanguinity. We must, therefore, acquiesce in the necessity, which denounces our Separation, and hold them, as we hold the rest of mankind, Enemies in War, in Peace Friends.

We, therefore, the Representatives of the united States of America, in General Congress, Assembled, appealing to the Supreme Judge of the world for the rectitude of our intentions, do, in the Name, and by Authority of the good People of these Colonies, solemnly publish and declare, That these United Colonies are, and of Right ought to be Free and Independent States; that they are Absolved from all Allegiance to the British Crown, and that all political connection between them and the State of Great Britain, is and ought to be totally dissolved; and that as Free and Independent States, they have full Power to levy War, conclude Peace, contract Alliances, establish Commerce, and to do all other Acts and Things which Independent States may of right do. And for the support of this Declaration, with a firm reliance on the Protection of Divine Providence, we mutually pledge to each other our Lives, our Fortunes and our sacred Honor.

JOHN HANCOCK.

New Hampshire—JOSIAH BARTLETT, WM. WHIPPLE, MATTHEW THORNTON.

Massachusetts Bay—SAML. ADAMS, JOHN ADAMS, ROBT. TREAT PAINE, ELBRIDGE GERRY.

Rhode Island—STEP. HOPKINS, WILLIAM ELLERY.

Connecticut—ROGER SHERMAN, SAM'EL HUNTINGTON, WM. WILLIAMS, OLIVER WOLCOTT.

New York—WM. FLOYD, PHIL. LIVINGSTON, FRANS. LEWIS, LEWIS MORRIS.

New Jersey—RICHD. STOCKTON, JNO. WITHERSPOON, FRAS. HOPKINSON, JOHN HART, ABRA. CLARK.

Pennsylvania — ROBT. MORRIS, BENJAMIN RUSH, BENJA. FRANKLIN, JOHN MORTON, GEO. CLYMER, JAS. SMITH, GEO. TAYLOR, JAMES WILSON, GEO. ROSS.

Delaware—CÆSAR RODNEY, GEO. READ, THO. M'KEAN.

Maryland—SAMUEL CHASE, WM. PACA, THOS. STONE, CHARLES CARROLL of Carrollton.

Virginia—GEORGE WYTHE, RICHARD HENRY LEE, TH. JEFFERSON, BENJA. HARRISON, THOS. NELSON, jr., FRANCIS LIGHTFOOT LEE, CARTER BRAXTON.

North Carolina—WM. HOOPER, JOSEPH HEWES, JOHN PENN.

South Carolina—EDWARD RUTLEDGE, THOS. HEYWARD, Junr., THOMAS LYNCH, Junr., ARTHUR MIDDLETON.

Georgia—BUTTON GWINNETT, LYMAN HALL, GEO. WALTON.

WASHINGTON'S
FAREWELL ADDRESS.

WASHINGTON AS A STATESMAN.

THE period during which Washington won his fame as a statesman extends from the time when he resigned his commission as commander-in-chief of the army, to his death in 1799. As this period recedes into the past, it is becoming more and more evident that no small part of his permanent fame will rest upon the sagacity, the penetration, and the tenacity of purpose which he displayed in this most exciting and critical period of our history. He was not a learned man as that term is generally understood, but he had made a collection of books on political science such as few private libraries of that day could equal. He had copied with his own hand an abstract, made by Madison, of the great authority on this subject at that time, Montesquieu's "Spirit of Laws."

After resigning his commission, he was invited to meet a committee of congress to assist in devising plans for establishing the government upon a peace basis. He suggested a series of measures which reveal his far-sightedness and his practical good sense. Among these, were the establishment of a military academy for the training of officers, the creation of a navy as a means of protecting our foreign commerce, and the outlines of a system for regulating our intercourse with Indian tribes. At a meeting of the commissioners of Virginia and Maryland at his house in 1785, he suggested that they should agree upon a uniform system of duties and other commercial regulations, and a uniform currency. This was the germ of the subsequent regulation of this whole subject by constitutional provision.

14

No one of the men at that time in public life had better opportunities for knowing, certainly no one was more profoundly convinced than Washington that the Confederation as a form of government was a failure. In view of the approaching disbanding of the army he wrote, June 8, 1783, a circular letter addressed to the Governors of the States but intended for the whole people, in which he says: " It is indispensable to the happiness of the individual States that there should be lodged somewhere a supreme power to regulate and govern the general concerns of the confederated republic, without which the union cannot be of long duration, and everything must very rapidly tend to anarchy and confusion. . . . It is only in our united character that we are known as an empire, that our independence is acknowledged, that our power can be regarded or our credit supported among foreign nations." And his letters as well as all his public acts show that all his great influence was wielded judiciously yet effectively for the formation of a federal union.

The purity of his character, his unselfish patriotism and his unparalleled services pointed him out as the one person above all others to preside over the Convention of 1787. At the suggestion of Franklin he was unanimously elected its president. Very delicate and difficult were the duties of the presiding officer of such a body of men, met for such a purpose. The permanent success of their work would have been hardly possible without the impartial, conciliating, magnanimous attitude of Washington through all the proceedings.

Whatever views may be entertained respecting the wisdom of his policy in regard to certain political measures, very few persons familiar with the period will now be disposed to question the fact that our present prosperity as a nation must be attributed, in no small degree, to the foresight, the prudence and the lofty patriotism with which for eight years he conducted the affairs of the government.

He rose above the narrow provincial politics of the day which distorted the judgment of some of the best men with whom he had been associated. His home policy showed that he grasped clearly the new idea of national existence, and

comprehended the measures best adapted to foster its feeble
life. He first lifted our foreign policy to an independent position. Accustomed for a century and a half to more or less
subserviency to foreign powers, "the great majority of the
people were either French or English," as an acute observer
remarked, "and but very few Americans." Washington saw
clearly that there was no safety for the new republic except in
a policy of neutrality. The determination to enforce this
policy would awaken a feeling of nationality, and compel the
respect of foreign powers. Once having adopted this course
he maintained it with an inflexible purpose in spite of violent
opposition and bitter abuse, until even his enemies were compelled to admit its wisdom.

Washington entered upon his duties as President with the
intention of being the President of the nation rather than of a
party. He was the more constrained to this course by reason
of his unanimous election.

If he did not wholly succeed in this patriotic endeavor, it is
because the successful administration of government under
conditions which at present exist is not possible except through
the organization of parties. None the less we cannot fail
to admire the lofty moral purpose that prompted him to
mediate between opposing parties and to rise above the petty
arts of the political aspirant. The attempt to maintain a
balance of parties in his cabinet, though plausible, was an
impracticable scheme, and on the retirement of Jefferson he
abandoned it. He made the mistake of thinking that the
political leaders of the day could act with as much freedom
from prejudice, and with as intense a desire for the common
welfare as himself. In these respects Washington stood alone.
It was this elevation above the plane of selfish motives that
gave him clearness of insight, and inspired the public mind
with such confidence in his leadership.

CRITICAL OPINIONS.

WASHINGTON stands alone and unapproachable like a snow-peak rising above its fellows into the clear air of morning, with a dignity, constancy and purity which have made him the ideal type of civic virtue to succeeding generations."—*Bryce, Am. Commonwealth*, I. 641.

" He did the two greatest things which in politics a man can have the privilege of attempting. He maintained by peace that independence of his country which he had acquired by war. He founded a free government in the name of the principles of order and by re-establishing their sway. Of all great men he was the most virtuous and the most fortunate. In the world God has no higher favors to bestow."—*Guizot's Essay on Washington*.

No truth can be uttered with more confidence than that his ends were always upright and his means always pure. He exhibits the rare example of a politician to whom wiles were absolutely unknown, and whose professions to foreign governments and to his own countrymen were always sincere. In him was fully exemplified the real distinction which forever exists between wisdom and cunning, and the importance as well as the truth of the maxim that ' honesty is the best policy.' "—*Marshall's Life of Washington*, Vol. II. 447.

THE FAREWELL ADDRESS.

For several years previous to the expiration of his second term, Washington had contemplated the preparation of such a paper. His purpose was to present the results of his observation and reflection upon the character of our institutions, and to utter such words of counsel as might befit the occasion.

It is well known that he consulted both Hamilton and Madison in the preparation of this address, and received valuable aid, not only in the way of suggestion, but of final revision, especially from the former. As to the share of Hamilton, the opinion of Jared Sparks may be quoted as offering a satisfactory explanation. "The question as to the manner in which the address originated is one of small moment since its real importance consists in being known to contain the sentiments of Washington, uttered on a solemn occasion and designed for the benefit of his countrymen. . . My opinion is that the address, in the shape it now bears, is much indebted for its language and style to the careful revision and skilful pen of Hamilton ; that he suggested some of the topics and amplified others, and that he undertook this task, not more as an act of friendship than from a sincere desire that a paper of this kind should go before the public in a form which would give it great and lasting utility. But I do not think that his aid, however valuable, was such as to detract from the substantial merit of Washington, or to divest him of a fair claim to the authorship of the address."

As a piece of literary workmanship, the address has just claims to be regarded as a classic, and may well serve as a model for statesmen in the preparation of state papers. In his letters and official papers Washington was accustomed to express himself with great clearness and directness and often with a certain felicity and grace of language. The address evidently comes from one who is aware that he has something important to say and tries to say it in simple and well-chosen words.

But the chief excellence of this document is due not so much to its literary merit as to its commanding moral and religious character. It is not addressed to statesmen and legislators but to the people. It sets forth the principles that lie at the basis of all permanent national prosperity, and insists upon the intimate relation between the character of a people and the perpetuity of their government. Never perhaps was the importance of morality and religion so thoroughly emphasized in any similar political document. Never were they commended to the practice of a people by any ruler with such affectionate earnestness. With all the fidelity of a counselor and friend, he points out the two evils which seemed to him most likely to imperil the safety of the nation—the danger from excessive party spirit and from foreign alliances. These were crying evils at that time, and had proved most serious obstacles to the wise administration of government. If our subsequent history has shown that he somewhat overestimated the latter of these dangers, yet on the other hand his manly words and example have done much to educate the people to appreciate their true position among the nations of the earth. But there is no trace of national narrowness or bigotry in his counsel. He commends a liberal and generous treatment of the rest of the world, quite in contrast with the sentiments and conduct that prevailed among the nations of Europe during the last century. It is this large and comprehensive view of things, a thoughtful consideration for others, heroic self-reliance, united with a true singleness of purpose that reveal the wise, fearless and truthful soul. The influence of this address upon the American people and indirectly upon foreign nations is a striking tribute to the supremacy of goodness. More enduring than mere intellectual greatness, such a character is destined to command the final homage of mankind.

Numerous editions of this address have been published, some of them at considerable expense. The original manuscript copy was purchased by James Lenox for twenty-five hundred dollars, and is now the possession of the Lenox Library, New York.

" As the generations have come and gone the farewell address has grown dearer to the hearts of the American people, and the children and the children's children of those to whom it was addressed have turned to it in all times, and have known that there was no room for error in following its counsel."—*Lodge's Life of Washington*, Vol. II. 245.

"If the farewell address saved us from this (a coalition with France) though it saved us from nothing else, it would deserve to be regarded as a blessing from Heaven through the counsels of Washington, not less in magnitude than the blessing of Independence which was vouchsafed to his sword."—*Horace Binney's Inquiry.*

REFERENCES.—In addition to the well-known Lives of Washington, the recent "Life" by Henry Cabot Lodge, in two volumes, in the *American Statesmen Series*, deserves careful study. Much of the political history of the period may be gathered from Marshall's Life. A truly adequate estimate of Washington cannot be formed without reading more or less of his correspondence, edited by Sparks, or in the more recent volumes of Ford, now in course of publication. A full discussion of Hamilton's share in the Address will be found in *Horace Binney's Inquiry.*

WASHINGTON'S FAREWELL ADDRESS

TO THE PEOPLE OF THE UNITED STATES.

FRIENDS AND FELLOW-CITIZENS :

The period for a new election of a citizen, to administer the executive government of the United States, being not far distant, and the time actually arrived, when your thoughts must be employed in designating the person, who is to be clothed with that important trust, it appears to me proper, especially as it may conduce to a more distinct expression of the public voice, that I should now apprize you of the resolution I have formed, to decline being considered among the number of those, out of whom a choice is to be made.

I beg you, at the same time, to do me the justice to be assured, that this resolution has not been taken without a strict regard to all the considerations appertaining to the relation, which binds a dutiful citizen to his country ; and that, in withdrawing the tender of service, which silence in my situation might imply, I am influenced by no diminution of zeal for your future interest ; no deficiency of grateful respect for your past kindness ; but am supported by a full conviction that the step is compatible with both.

The acceptance of, and continuance hitherto in, the office to which your suffrages have twice called me, have been a uniform sacrifice of inclination to the opinion of duty, and to a deference for what appeared to be your desire. I constantly hoped, that it would have been much earlier in my power, consistently with motives, which I was not at liberty to disregard, to return to that retirement, from which I had been reluctantly drawn. The strength of my inclination to do this, previous to the last election, had even led to the preparation of an address to declare it to you ; but mature reflection on the then perplexed and critical posture of our affairs with foreign nations, and the unanimous advice of persons entitled to my confidence, impelled me to abandon the idea.

I rejoice, that the state of your concerns, external as well as internal, no longer renders the pursuit of inclination incompatible with the sentiment of duty, or propriety ; and am persuaded, whatever partiality may be retained for my services, that, in the present circumstances of our country, you will not disapprove my determination to retire.

The impressions, with which I first undertook the arduous trust, were explained on the proper occasion. In the discharge of this trust, I will only say, that I have, with good intentions, contributed towards the organization and administration of the government the best exertions of which a very fallible judgment was capable. Not, unconscious, in the outset, of the inferiority of my qualifications, experience in my own eyes, perhaps still more in the eyes of others, has strengthened the motives to diffidence of myself ; and every day the increasing weight of years admonishes me more and more, that the shade of retirement is as necessary to me as it will be welcome. Satisfied, that, if any circumstances have given peculiar value to my services, they were temporary, I have the consolation to believe, that, while choice and prudence invite me to quit the political scene, patriotism does not forbid it.

In looking forward to the moment, which is intended to terminate the career of my public life, my feelings do not permit me to suspend the deep acknowledgment of that debt of gratitude, which I owe to my beloved country for the many honors it has conferred upon me ; still more for the steadfast confidence with which it has supported me ; and for the opportunities I have thence enjoyed of manifesting my inviolable attachment, by services faithful and persevering, though in usefulness unequal to my zeal. If benefits have resulted to our country from these services, let it always be remembered to your praise, and as an instructive example in our annals, that under circumstances in which the passions, agitated in every direction, were liable to mislead, amidst appearances sometimes dubious, vicissitudes of fortune often discouraging, in situations in which not unfrequently want of success has countenanced the spirit of criticism, the constancy of your support was the essential prop of the efforts, and a guarantee

of the plans by which they were effected. Profoundly pene-
trated with this idea, I shall carry it with me to my grave, as
a strong incitement to unceasing vows that Heaven may continue to you the choicest tokens of its beneficence ; that your
union and brotherly affection may be perpetual ; that the free
constitution, which is the work of your hands, may be sacredly
maintained ; that its administration in every department may
be stamped with wisdom and virtue ; that, in fine, the happiness of the people of these States, under the auspices of liberty, may be made complete, by so careful a preservation and
so prudent a use of this blessing, as will acquire to them the
glory of recommending it to the applause, the affection, and
adoption of every nation, which is yet a stranger to it.

Here, perhaps, I ought to stop. But a solicitude for your
welfare, which cannot end but with my life, and the apprehension of danger, natural to that solicitude, urge me, on an
occasion like the present, to offer to your solemn contemplation, and to recommend to your frequent review, some sentiments, which are the result of much reflection, of no inconsid-
erable observation, and which appear to me all-important to
the permanency of your felicity as a People. These will be
offered to you with the more freedom, as you can only see in
them the disinterested warnings of a parting friend, who can
possibly have no personal motive to bias his counsel. Nor can
I forget, as an encouragement to it, your indulgent reception
of my sentiments on a former and not dissimilar occasion.

Interwoven as is the love of liberty with every ligament of
your hearts, no recommendation of mine is necessary to fortify
or confirm the attachment.

The unity of Government, which constitutes you one people, is also now dear to you. It is justly so : for it is a main
pillar in the edifice of your real independence, the support of
your tranquillity at home, your peace abroad ; of your safety;
of your prosperity ; of that very Liberty, which you so highly
prize. But as it is easy to foresee, that, from different causes
and from different quarters, much pains will be taken, many
artifices employed, to weaken in your minds the conviction of
this truth ; as this is the point in your political fortress against

which the batteries of internal and external enemies will be most constantly and actively (though often covertly and insidiously) directed, it is of infinite moment, that you should properly estimate the immense value of your national Union to your collective and individual happiness ; that you should cherish a cordial, habitual, and immovable attachment to it ; accustoming yourselves to think and speak of it as of the Palladium of your political safety and prosperity ; watching for its preservation with jealous anxiety ; discountenancing whatever may suggest even a suspicion, that it can in any event be abandoned ; and indignantly frowning upon the first dawning of every attempt to alienate any portion of our country from the rest, or to enfeeble the sacred ties which now link together the various parts.

For this you have every inducement of sympathy and interest. Citizens, by birth or choice, of a common country, that country has a right to concentrate your affections. The name of AMERICAN, which belongs to you, in your national capacity, must always exalt the just pride of Patriotism, more than any appellation derived from local discriminations. With slight shades of difference, you have the same religion, manners, habits, and political principles. You have in a common cause fought and triumphed together ; the Independence and Liberty you possess are the work of joint counsels, and joint efforts, of common dangers, sufferings, and successes.

But these considerations, however powerfully they address themselves to your sensibility, are greatly outweighed by those, which apply more immediately to your interest. Here, every portion of our country finds the most commanding motives for carefully guarding and preserving the Union of the whole.

The *North*, in an unrestrained intercourse with the *South*, protected by the equal laws of a common government, finds, in the productions of the latter, great additional resources of maritime and commercial enterprise and precious materials of manufacturing industry. The *South*, in the same intercourse, benefiting by the agency of the *North*, sees its agriculture grow and its commerce expand. Turning partly into its own channels the seamen of the *North*, it finds its particular navigation invigorated ; and, while it contributes, in different ways, to nourish and increase the general mass of the national navigation, it looks forward to the protection of a maritime strength, to which itself is unequally adapted. The *East*, in a like intercourse with the *West*, already finds, and in the progressive improvement of interior communications by land and water, will more and more find, a valuable vent for the commodities which it brings from abroad, or manufactures at home. The *West* derives from the *East* supplies requisite to its growth and comfort, and, what is perhaps of still greater consequence, it must of necessity owe the *secure* enjoyment of indispensable *outlets* for its own productions to the weight, influence, and the future maritime strength of the Atlantic side of the Union, directed by an indissoluble community of interest as *one nation*. Any other tenure by which the *West* can hold this essential advantage, whether derived from its own separate strength, or from an apostate and unnatural connection with any foreign power, must be intrinsically precarious.

While, then, every part of our country thus feels an immediate and particular interest in Union, all the parts combined cannot fail to find in the united mass of means and efforts greater strength, greater resource, proportionably greater security from external danger, a less frequent interruption of their peace by foreign nations ; and, what is of inestimable value, they must derive from Union an exemption from those broils and wars between themselves, which so frequently afflict neighboring countries not tied together by the same governments, which their own rivalships alone would be sufficient to produce, but which opposite foreign alliances, attachments, and intrigues would stimulate and embitter. Hence, likewise, they will avoid the necessity of those overgrown military establishments, which, under any form of government, are inauspicious to liberty, and which are to be regarded as particularly hostile to Republican Liberty. In this sense it is, that your Union ought to be considered as a main prop of your liberty, and that the love of the one ought to endear to you the preservation of the other.

These considerations speak a persuasive language to every reflecting and virtuous mind, and exhibit the continuance of the UNION as a primary object of Patriotic desire. Is there a doubt, whether a common government can embrace so large a sphere? Let experience solve it. To listen to mere speculation in such a case were criminal. We are authorized to hope, that a proper organization of the whole, with the auxiliary agency of governments for the respective subdivisions, will afford a happy issue to the experiment. It is well worth a fair and full experiment. With such powerful and obvious motives to Union, affecting all parts of our country, while experience shall not have demonstrated its impracticability, there will always be reason to distrust the patriotism of those, who in any quarter may endeavor to weaken its bands.

In contemplating the causes, which may disturb our Union, it occurs as matter of serious concern, that any ground should have been furnished for characterizing parties by *Geographical* discriminations, *Northern* and *Southern*, *Atlantic* and *Western;* whence designing men may endeavor to excite a belief, that there is a real difference of local interests and views. One of the expedients of party to acquire influence, within particular districts, is to misrepresent the opinions and aims of other districts. You cannot shield yourselves too much against the jealousies and heart-burnings, which spring from these misrepresentations ; they tend to render alien to each other those, who ought to be bound together by fraternal affection. The inhabitants of our western country have lately had a useful lesson on this head ; they have seen, in the negotiation by the Executive, and in the unanimous ratification by the Senate, of the treaty with Spain, and in the universal satisfaction at that event, throughout the United States, a decisive proof how unfounded were the suspicions propagated among them of a policy in the General Government and in the Atlantic States unfriendly to their interests in regard to the MISSISSIPPI ; they have been witnesses to the formation of two treaties, that with Great Britain, and that with Spain, which secure to them every thing they could desire, in respect to our foreign relations, towards confirming their prosperity. Will it not be their wisdom to rely for the preservation of these advantages on the UNION by which they were procured? Will they not henceforth be deaf to those advisers, if such there are, who would sever them from their brethren, and connect them with aliens?

To the efficacy and permanency of your Union, a Government for the whole is indispensable. No alliances, however strict, between the parts can be an adequate substitute; they must inevitably experience the infractions and interruptions, which all alliances in all times have experienced. Sensible of this momentous truth, you have improved upon your first essay, by the adoption of a Constitution of Government better calculated than your former for an intimate Union, and for the efficacious management of your common concerns. This Government, the offspring of our own choice, uninfluenced and unawed, adopted upon full investigation and mature deliberation, completely free in its principles, in the distribution of its powers, uniting security with energy, and containing within itself a provision for its own amendment, has a just claim to your confidence and your support. Respect for its authority, compliance with its laws, acquiescence in its measures, are duties enjoined by the fundamental maxims of true Liberty. The basis of our political systems is the right of the people to make and to alter their Constitutions of Government. But the Constitution which at any time exists, till changed by an explicit and authentic act of the whole people, is sacredly obligatory upon all. The very idea of the power and the right of the people to establish Government presupposes the duty of every individual to obey the established Government.

All obstructions to the execution of the Laws, all combinations and associations, under whatever plausible character, with the real design to direct, control, counteract, or awe the regular deliberation and action of the constituted authorities, are destructive of this fundamental principle, and of fatal tendency. They serve to organize faction, to give it an artificial and extraordinary force; to put, in the place of the delegated will of the nation, the will of a party, often a small but artful and enterprising minority of the community; and, according to the alternate triumphs of different parties, to make the public administration the mirror of the ill-concerted and incongruous projects of faction, rather than the organ of consistent and wholesome plans digested by common counsels, and modified by mutual interests.

However combinations or associations of the above descriptions may now and then answer popular ends, they are likely in the course of time and things, to become potent engines, by which cunning, ambitious, and unprincipled men will be enabled to subvert the power of the people, and to usurp for themselves the reins of government ; destroying afterwards the very engines, which have lifted them to unjust dominion.

Towards the preservation of your government, and the permanency of your present happy state, it is requisite, not only that you steadily discountenance irregular oppositions to its acknowledged authority, but also that you resist with care the spirit of innovation upon its principles, however specious the pretexts. One method of assault may be to effect, in the forms of the constitution, alterations, which will impair the energy of the system, and thus to undermine what cannot be directly overthrown. In all the changes to which you may be invited, remember that time and habit are at least as necessary to fix the true character of governments, as of other human institutions ; that experience is the surest standard, by which to test the real tendency of the existing constitution of a country ; that facility in changes, upon the credit of mere hypothesis and opinion, exposes to perpetual change, from the endless variety of hypothesis and opinion ; and remember, especially, that, for the efficient management of your common interests, in a country so extensive as ours, a government of as much vigor as is consistent with the perfect security of liberty is indispensable. Liberty itself will find in such a government, with powers properly distributed and adjusted, its surest guardian. It is, indeed, little else than a name, where the government is too feeble to withstand the enterprise of faction, to confine each member of the society within the limits prescribed by the laws, and to maintain all in the secure and tranquil enjoyment of the rights of person and property.

I have already intimated to you the danger of parties in the state, with particular reference to the founding of them on geographical discriminations. Let me now take a more comprehensive view, and warn you in the most solemn manner against the baneful effects of the spirit of party, generally.

This spirit, unfortunately, is inseparable from our nature, having its root in the strongest passions of the human mind. It exists under different shapes in all governments, more or less stifled, controlled, or repressed ; but, in those of the popular form, it is seen in its greatest rankness, and is truly their worst enemy.

The alternate domination of one faction over another, sharpened by the spirit of revenge, natural to party dissension, which in different ages and countries has perpetrated the most horrid enormities, is itself a frightful despotism. But this leads at length to a more formal and permanent despotism. The disorders and miseries, which result, gradually incline the minds of men to seek security and repose in the absolute power of an individual ; and sooner or later the chief of some prevailing faction, more able or more fortunate than his competitors, turns this disposition to the purposes of his own elevation, on the ruins of Public Liberty.

Without looking forward to an extremity of this kind (which nevertheless ought not to be entirely out of sight), the common and continual mischiefs of the spirit of party are sufficient to make it the interest and duty of a wise people to discourage and restrain it.

It serves always to distract the Public Councils, and enfeeble the Public Administration. It agitates the Community with ill-founded jealousies and false alarms ; kindles the animosity of one party against another, foments occasionally riot and insurrection. It opens the door to foreign influence and corruption, which find a facilitated access to the government itself through the channels of party passions. Thus the policy and the will of one country are subjected to the policy and will of another.

There is an opinion, that parties in free countries are useful checks upon the administration of the Government, and serve to keep alive the spirit of Liberty. This within certain limits is probably true ; and in Governments of a Monarchical cast, Patriotism may look with indulgence, if not with favor, upon the spirit of party. But in those of the popular character, in Governments purely elective, it is a spirit not to be encouraged. From their natural tendency, it is certain there will always be enough of that spirit for every salutary purpose. And, there being constant danger of excess, the effort ought to be, by force of public opinion, to mitigate and assuage it. A fire not to be quenched, it demands a uniform vigilance to prevent its bursting into a flame, lest, instead of warming, it should consume.

It is important, likewise, that the habits of thinking in a free country should inspire caution, in those intrusted with its administration, to confine themselves within their respective constitutional spheres, avoiding in the exercise of the powers of one department to encroach upon another. The spirit of encroachment tends to consolidate the powers of all the departments in one, and thus to create, whatever the form of government, a real despotism. A just estimate of that love of power, and proneness to abuse it, which predominates in the human heart, is sufficient to satisfy us of the truth of this position. The necessity of reciprocal checks in the exercise of political power, by dividing and distributing it into different depositories, and constituting each the Guardian of the Public Weal against invasions by the others, has been evinced by experiments ancient and modern ; some of them in our country and under our own eyes. To preserve them must be as necessary as to institute them. If, in the opinion of the people, the distribution or modification of the constitutional powers be in any particular wrong, let it be corrected by an amendment in the way, which the constitution designates. But let there be no change by usurpation ; for, though this, in one instance, may be the instrument of good, it is the customary weapon by which free governments are destroyed. The precedent must always greatly overbalance in permanent evil any partial or transient benefit, which the use can at any time yield.

Of all the dispositions and habits, which lead to political prosperity, Religion and Morality are indispensable supports. In vain would that man claim the tribute of Patriotism, who should labor to subvert these great pillars of human happiness, these firmest props of the duties of Men and Citizens. The mere Politician, equally with the pious man, ought to respect and to cherish them. A volume could not trace all their connections with private and public felicity. Let it simply be asked, Where is the security for property, for reputation, for life, if the sense of religious obligation *desert* the oaths, which are the instruments of investigation in Courts of Justice? And let us with caution indulge the supposition, that morality can be maintained without religion. Whatever may be conceded to the influence of refined education on minds of peculiar structure, reason and experience both forbid us to expect, that national morality can prevail in exclusion of religious principle.

It is substantially true, that virtue or morality is a necessary spring of popular government. The rule, indeed, extends with more or less force to every species of free government. Who, that is a sincere friend to it, can look with indifference upon attempts to shake the foundation of the fabric?

Promote, then, as an object of primary importance, institutions for the general diffusion of knowledge. In proportion as the structure of a government gives force to public opinion, it is essential that public opinion should be enlightened.

As a very important source of strength and security, cherish public credit. One method of preserving it is, to use it as sparingly as possible; avoiding occasions of expense by cultivating peace, but remembering also that timely disbursements to prepare for danger frequently prevent much greater disbursements to repel it; avoiding likewise the accumulation of debt, not only by shunning occasions of expense, but by vigorous exertions in time of peace to discharge the debts, which unavoidable wars may have occasioned, not ungenerously throwing upon posterity the burthen, which we ourselves ought to bear. The execution of these maxims belongs to your representatives, but it is necessary that public opinion should coöperate. To facilitate to them the performance of their duty, it is essential that you should practically bear in mind, that towards the payment of debts there must be Revenue; that to have Revenue there must be taxes; that no taxes can be devised, which are not more or less inconvenient and unpleasant, that the intrinsic embarrassment, inseparable from the selection of the proper objects (which is always a choice of difficulties), ought to be a decisive motive for a candid construction of the conduct of the government in making it, and for a spirit of acquiescence in the measures for obtaining revenue, which the public exigencies may at any time dictate.

Observe good faith and justice towards all Nations; cultivate peace and harmony with all. Religion and Morality enjoin this conduct; and can it be, that good policy does not equally enjoin it? It will be worthy of a free, enlightened, and, at no distant period, a great Nation, to give to mankind the magnanimous and too novel example of a people always guided by an exalted justice and benevolence. Who can doubt, that, in the course of time and things, the fruits of such a plan would richly repay any temporary advantages, which might be lost by a steady adherence to it? Can it be, that Providence has not connected the permanent felicity of a Nation with its Virtue? The experiment, at least, is recommended by every sentiment which ennobles human nature. Alas! is it rendered impossible by its vices?

In the execution of such a plan, nothing is more essential, than that permanent, inveterate antipathies against particular Nations, and passionate attachments for others, should be excluded; and that, in place of them, just and amicable feelings towards all should be cultivated. The Nation, which indulges towards another an habitual hatred, or an habitual fondness, is in some degree a slave. It is a slave to its animosity or to its affection, either of which is sufficient to lead it astray from its duty and its interest. Antipathy in one nation against another disposes each more readily to offer insult and injury, to lay hold of slight causes of umbrage, and to be haughty and intractable, when accidental or trifling occasions of dispute occur. Hence frequent collisions, obstinate, envenomed, and bloody contests. The Nation, prompted by ill-will and resentment, sometimes impels to war the Government, contrary to the best calculations of policy. The Government sometimes participates in the national propensity, and adopts through passion what reason would reject ; at other times, it makes the animosity of the nation subservient to projects of hostility instigated by pride, ambition, and other sinister and pernicious motives. The peace often, sometimes perhaps the liberty, of Nations has been the victim.

So likewise, a passionate attachment of one Nation for another produces a variety of evils. Sympathy for the favorite Nation, facilitating the illusion of an imaginary common interest, in cases where no real common interest exists, and infusing into one the enmities of the other, betrays the former into a participation in the quarrels and wars of the latter, without adequate inducement or justification. It leads also to concessions to the favorite Nation of privileges denied to others, which is apt doubly to injure the Nation making the concessions ; by unnecessarily parting with what ought to have been retained ; and by exciting jealousy, ill-will, and a disposition to retaliate, in the parties from whom equal privileges are withheld. And it gives to ambitious, corrupted, or deluded citizens (who devote themselves to the favorite nation), facility to betray or sacrifice the interests of their own country, without odium, sometimes even with popularity ; gilding, with the appearances of a virtuous sense of obligation, a commendable deference for public opinion, or a laudable zeal for public good, the base of foolish compliances of ambition, corruption, or infatuation.

As avenues to foreign influence in innumerable ways, such attachments are particularly alarming to the truly enlightened and independent Patriot. How many opportunities do they afford to tamper with domestic factions, to practice the arts of seduction, to mislead public opinion, to influence or awe the Public Councils ! Such an attachment of a small or weak, towards a great and powerful nation, dooms the former to be the satellite of the latter.

Against the insidious wiles of foreign influence (I conjure you to believe me, fellow citizens), the jealousy of a free people ought to be *constantly* awake ; since history and experience prove, that foreign influence is one of the most baneful foes of Republican Government. But that jealousy, to be useful, must be impartial ; else it becomes the instrument of the very influence to be avoided, instead of a defense against it. Excessive partiality for one foreign nation, and excessive dislike of another, cause those whom they actuate to see danger only on one side, and serve to veil and even second the arts of influence on the other. Real patriots, who may resist the intrigues of the favorite, are liable to become suspected and odious ; while its tools and dupes usurp the applause and confidence of the people, to surrender their interests.

The great rule of conduct for us, in regard to foreign nations, is, in extending our commercial relations, to have with them as little *political* connection as possible. So far as we have already formed engagements, let them be fulfilled with perfect good faith. Here let us stop.

Europe has a set of primary interests, which to us have none, or a very remote relation. Hence she must be engaged in frequent controversies, the causes of which are essentially foreign to our concerns. Hence, therefore, it must be unwise in us to implicate ourselves, by artificial ties, in the ordinary vicissitudes of her politics, or the ordinary combinations and collisions of her friendships or enmities.

Our detached and distant situation invites and enables us to pursue a different course. If we remain one people, under an efficient government, the period is not far off, when we may defy material injury from external annoyance ; when we may take such an attitude as will cause the neutrality, we may at any time resolve upon, to be scrupulously respected ; when belligerent nations, under the impossibility of making acquisitions upon us, will not lightly hazard the giving us provocation ; when we may choose peace or war, as our interest, guided by justice, shall counsel.

Why forego the advantages of so peculiar a situation ? Why quit our own to stand upon foreign ground ? Why, by interweaving our destiny with that of any part of Europe, entangle our peace and prosperity in the toils of European ambition, rivalship, interest, humor, or caprice ?

It is our true policy to steer clear of permanent alliances with any portion of the foreign world ; so far, I mean, as we are now at liberty to do it ; for let me not be understood as capable of patronizing infidelity to existing engagements. I hold the maxim no less applicable to public than to private affairs, that honesty is always the best policy. I repeat it, therefore, let those engagements be observed in their genuine sense. But, in my opinion, it is unnecessary and would be unwise to extend them.

Taking care always to keep ourselves, by suitable establishments, on a respectable defensive posture, we may safely trust to temporary alliances for extraordinary emergencies.

Harmony, liberal intercourse with all nations, are recommended by policy, humanity, and interest. But even our commercial policy should hold an equal and impartial hand ; neither seeking nor granting exclusive favors or preferences ; consulting the natural course of things ; diffusing and diversifying by gentle means the streams of commerce, but forcing nothing ; establishing, with powers so disposed, in order to give trade a stable course, to define the rights of our merchants, and to enable the government to support them, conventional rules of intercourse, the best that present circumstances and mutual opinion will permit, but temporary, and liable to be from time to time abandoned or varied, as experience and circumstances shall dictate ; constantly keeping in view, that it is folly in one nation to look for disinterested favors from another ; that it must pay with a portion of its independence for whatever it may accept under that character ; that, by such acceptance, it may place itself in the condition of having given equivalents for nominal favors, and yet of being reproached with ingratitude for not giving more. There can be no greater error than to expect or calculate upon real favors from nation to nation. It is an illusion, which experience must cure, which a just pride ought to discard.

In offering to you, my countrymen, these counsels of an old and affectionate friend, I dare not hope they will make the strong and lasting impression I could wish; that they will control the usual current of the passions, or prevent our nation from running the course, which has hitherto marked the destiny of nations. But, if I may even flatter myself, that they may be productive of some partial benefit, some occasional good; that they may now and then recur to moderate the fury of party spirit, to warn against the mischiefs of foreign intrigue, to guard against the impostures of pretended patriotism; this hope will be a full recompense for the solicitude for your welfare, by which they have been dictated.

How far in the discharge of my official duties, I have been guided by the principles which have been delineated, the public records and other evidences of my conduct must witness to you and to the world. To myself, the assurance of my own conscience is, that I have at least believed myself to be guided by them.

In relating to the still subsisting war in Europe, my Proclamation of the 22d of April, 1793, is the index of my Plan. Sanctioned by your approving voice, and by that of your Representatives in both Houses of Congress, the spirit of that measure has continually governed me, uninfluenced by any attempts to deter or divert me from it.

After deliberate examination, with the aid of the best lights I could obtain, I was well satisfied that our country, under all the circumstances of the case, had a right to take, and was bound in duty and interest to take, a neutral position. Having taken it, I determined, as far as should depend upon me, to maintain it, with moderation, perseverance, and firmness.

The considerations, which respect the right to hold this conduct, it is not necessary on this occasion to detail. I will only observe, that, according to my understanding of the matter, that right, so far from being denied by any of the Belligerent Powers, has been virtually admitted by all.

The duty of holding a neutral conduct may be inferred, without anything more, from the obligation which justice and humanity impose on every nation, in cases in which it is free to act, to maintain inviolate the relations of peace and amity towards other nations.

The inducements of interest for observing that conduct will best be referred to your own reflections and experience. With me, a predominant motive has been to endeavor to gain time to our country to settle and mature its yet recent institutions, and to progress without interruption to that degree of strength and consistency, which is necessary to give it, humanly speaking, the command of its own fortunes.

Though, in reviewing the incidents of my administration, I am unconscious of intentional error, I am nevertheless too sensible of my defects not to think it probable that I may have committed many errors. Whatever they may be, I fervently beseech the Almighty to avert or mitigate the evils to which they may tend. I shall also carry with me the hope, that my Country will never cease to view them with indulgence; and that, after forty-five years of my life dedicated to its service with an upright zeal, the faults of incompetent abilities will be consigned to oblivion, as myself must soon be to the mansions of rest.

Relying on its kindness in this as in other things, and actuated by that fervent love towards it, which is so natural to a man, who views in it the native soil of himself and his progenitors for several generations ; I anticipate with pleasing expectation that retreat, in which I promise myself to realize, without alloy, the sweet enjoyment of partaking, in the midst of my fellow-citizens, the benign influence of good laws under a free government, the ever favorite object of my heart, and the happy reward, as I trust, of our mutual cares, labors, and dangers.   GEORGE WASHINGTON.

United States, September 17th, 1796.

LINCOLN'S INAUGURATION.

THE ELECTION OF PRESIDENT LINCOLN.

On the sixth day of November, 1860, Abraham Lincoln was elected President of the United States. For the fifteen years preceding, the country had been in a state of constant agitation respecting the question of the extension of slavery. The Mexican War, the admission of Texas, the admission of California, the Repeal of the Missouri Compromise, the conflict in Kansas and Nebraska, the Dred Scott Decision were all phases of a struggle which had been growing more intense and bitter and which had awakened painful forebodings in all patriotic hearts. The South had grown bold and aggressive. It was determined to maintain an equal representation in the senate with the North. This would be impossible without the admission of more slave states. On the other hand the idea that the ownership of one man by another was a moral wrong, that it brought degradation to both master and slave and that therefore the system which was identified with the spread of these evils must be "cribbed, cabined, and confined," had been taking a deeper hold of the public conscience in the North. Hence men talked of an "irrepressible conflict." The national outcome was the formation of the Republican party in 1856, whose cardinal principle was opposition to the extension of slavery in the territories. On this issue Mr. Lincoln had won an election to the senate of the United States after a most exciting contest with Judge Douglas. In this great senatorial contest he had shown himself to be not only a very able debater and a wise politician, but a man of earnest convictions and firm principles. This event had, doubtless, an important influence in securing his nomination for the presidency in 1860. The election resulted in the choice of Mr. Lincoln by a popular vote greater than any President had ever before received. The four months interven-

38

ing between his election and inauguration were full of the most stirring events. Beginning with South Carolina seven states had passed Ordinances of secession and met Feb. 4th at Montgomery, Ala., to form a Confederacy. The ostensible reason for this movement was presented by the Governor of South Carolina, who justified it on the ground that "in the recent election for President and Vice-President, the North had carried the election upon principles that make it no longer safe for us to rely upon the powers of the Federal Government or the guarantees of the Federal Compact." But other leaders in the Confederacy had the frankness to avow that this was not a spasmodic movement, but the result of a long cherished purpose. After his election to the vice-presidency of the Confederacy Mr. Stephens found the real reason for the movement to be "that it has put at rest forever all agitating questions relating to our peculiar institutions . . . . the proper *status* of the negro in our form of civilization." Meanwhile several members of Pres. Buchanan's cabinet had resigned their positions, the senators from the seceding states had left their seats in Congress and the forts, arsenals, and other public property of the United States within the limits of the Confederacy had been seized. The session of Congress had been wasted in futile attempts to conciliate the South by the passage of various resolutions, and amendments to the Constitution. As a pledge of their intention not to interfere with slavery they had adopted a Resolution to amend the constitution, prohibiting forever any amendment of the same interfering with slavery in any State.

Mr. Buchanan had declined to interfere with any movements looking to the establishment of an independent government in the South. Officers of the army and navy were entering the Confederate service and extensive preparations were being made for the reduction of Fort Sumter. The closing weeks of the administration were multiplying the difficulties that would beset the assumption of the presidential office by his successor. Mr. Lincoln did not exaggerate the fact in saying that those duties were " greater than had devolved upon any other man since the days of Washington."

THE INAUGURAL ADDRESS.

MR. LINCOLN had arrived in Washington February 23d. On his way from Springfield, Ill., he had addressed attentive crowds, in all the large cities as far east as Albany, upon the topics that were then uppermost in the minds of all men. These addresses were full of loyalty to the Union, of unbounded confidence in the people and expressed the most devout desire for divine guidance and support.

The latter part of his journey had been hastened by the discovery of a plot intended to prevent his reaching the Capital. His friends had thought best to frustrate this plot by a sudden change of plan. It was with a feeling of relief that the people learned of his safe arrival in Washington.

According to the usual custom the ceremony of inauguration took place in front of the Capitol. The constitutional oath was administered by Chief Justice Taney, who three years before had framed the Dred Scott Decision. Judge Douglas stood by his side and held his hat. The address was delivered in presence of an immense multitude of spectators, and of a large military force under the command of General Scott. It was listened to with profound attention, and all the passages which contained any allusion to the Union were heartily cheered.

The address in almost every line reveals the manner of one who proposes to meet a grave crisis by an appeal to the noblest sentiments of our nature—an appeal to reason and to patriotism. The language is dignified, direct, and devoid of ornament except in the concluding paragraph which is strikingly figurative and exquisitely finished. There runs through it a certain tone of respectful friendliness to the South. With a spirit of evident sincerity. he repels the charge that his election was likely to endanger the personal security or the property of the people of the South. Appealing to his previous utterances, and to the platform of the party which has elected him, he re-asserts his intention to administer the constitution and the laws as the yare, "with no mental reservations and with no purpose to construe the constitution by any hypercritical rules." With equal frankness he states his views upon the subject of secession, and declares his intention to maintain the authority of the government "over all property and places belonging to it."

In a few tersely written paragraphs he proceeds to set forth the fundamental principles upon which our government rests—that it is essentially a government of the majority, and yet of a majority held in restraint by checks which protect the rights of the minority; that neither the President, Congress, nor the Supreme Court is invested with any sovereignty, but must derive all authority from the people; and that accordingly when conflicting opinions arise as to the interpretation of the Constitution, the true remedy is not the secession of the aggrieved party but the submission of the whole matter to the people, who are competent to amend their own instrument of government. It is doubtful whether in the whole range of our political literature a more admirable statement of the essential features of our government can be found in the same number of lines.

Evidently oppressed by a solemn sense of the momentous results of their decision, Mr. Lincoln counsels the dissatisfied to deliberate calmly and avoid precipitate action. Intelligence, patriotism and piety "are still competent to adjust, in the best way, all our present difficulties." The address closes in a strain of touching pathos happily adapted to allay all sectional feeling and to stir the liveliest sentiments of patriotism in every American heart.

CRITICAL ESTIMATES.

"Mr. Lincoln was not an agitator like Garrison, Phillips, and O'Connell, and as a reformer he belonged to the class of moderate men, such as Peel and Gladstone; but in no condition did he ever confound right with wrong, or speak of injustice with bated breath. His first printed paper was a plea for temperance, his second a eulogy upon the Union."—*Geo. Boutwell in Rice's Reminiscences of Lincoln.*

"Mr. Lincoln professed to wait on events or rather on the manifestation of the moral forces around him, wherein with a mind sobered by responsibility and unclouded by selfishness he earnestly endeavored to read the will of God, which, having read, he patiently followed to the best of his power."—*Goldwin Smith, in McMillan's Magazine.*

No higher compliment was ever paid to a nation than the simple confidence, the fireside plainness with which Mr. Lincoln always addresses the reason of the American people. This was indeed a true democrat who grounded himself on the assumption that a democracy can think. "Come, let us reason together about this matter" has been the tone of all his addresses to the people ; and accordingly we have never had a chief magistrate who so won to himself the love and, at the same time, the judgment of his countrymen.—*Lowell, My Study Windows, p.* 174.

Standing above the loose morality of party politics, standing above the maxims and conventionalisms of statesmanship, leaving aside all indirections and insincerities of diplomacy, trusting the people, leaning upon the people, inspired by the people who, in their Christian homes and Christian sanctuaries gave it their confidence, the administration of Abraham Lincoln stands out in history as the finest exhibition of a Christian democracy the world has ever seen.—*Holland's Life of Lincoln, p.* 542.

REFERENCES.—Very good accounts of the public and private life of Mr. Lincoln may be found in " Raymond's History of the Administration of Abraham Lincoln," Holland's, Arnold's, and Lamon's Lives—the latter giving more of his history before he became President. These should be compared with the Nicolay-Hay life that has for some time been appearing in the *Century,* and also with a recent volume of the " Personal Recollections of Lincoln," by Herndon.

LINCOLN'S FIRST INAUGURAL, THE EMANCIPATION PROCLAMATION, AND THE GETTYSBURG ADDRESS.

FIRST INAUGURAL ADDRESS.

March 4, 1861.

FELLOW-CITIZENS OF THE UNITED STATES :

In compliance with a custom as old as the government itself, I appear before you to address you briefly, and to take, in your presence, the oath prescribed by the Constitution of the United States to be taken by the President before he enters on the execution of his office.

I do not consider it necessary, at present, for me to discuss those matters of administration about which there is no special anxiety or excitement. Apprehension seems to exist among the people of the southern states, that, by the accession of a republican administration, their property and their peace and personal security are to be endangered. There has never been any reasonable cause for such apprehension. Indeed, the most ample evidence to the contrary has all the while existed and been open to their inspection. It is found in nearly all the published speeches of him who now addresses you. I do but quote from one of those speeches, when I declare that "I have no purpose, directly or indirectly, to interfere with the institution of slavery in the states where it exists." I believe I have no lawful right to do so ; and I have no inclination to do so. Those who nominated and elected me did so with the full knowledge that I had made this, and made many similar declarations, and had never recanted them. And, more than this, they placed in the platform, for my acceptance, and as a law to themselves and to me, the clear and emphatic resolution which I now read :

"*Resolved*, That the maintenance inviolate of the rights of the states, and especially the right of each state to order and control its own domestic institutions according to its own judgment exclusively, is essential to that balance of power on which the perfection and endurance of our political fabric depend ;

and we denounce the lawless invasion by armed force of the soil of any state or territory, no matter under what pretext, as among the gravest of crimes."

I now reiterate these sentiments; and in doing so I only press upon the public attention the most conclusive evidence of which the case is susceptible, that the property, peace, and security of no section are to be in anywise endangered by the now incoming administration.

I add, too, that all the protection which, consistently with the Constitution and the laws, can be given, will be cheerfully given to all the states when lawfully demanded, for whatever cause, as cheerfully to one section as to another.

There is much controversy about the delivering up of fugitives from service or labor. The clause I now read is as plainly written in the Constitution as any other of its provisions:

"No person held to service or labor in one state under the laws thereof, escaping into another, shall, in consequence of any law or regulation therein, be discharged from such service or labor, but shall be delivered up on claim of the party to whom such service or labor may be due."

It is scarcely questioned that this provision was intended by those who made it for the reclaiming of what we call fugitive slaves; and the intention of the law-giver is the law.

All members of Congress swear their support to the whole Constitution—to this provision as well as any other. To the proposition, then, that slaves whose cases come within the terms of this clause "shall be delivered up," their oaths are unanimous. Now, if they would make the effort in good temper, could they not, with nearly equal unanimity, frame and pass a law by means of which to keep good that unanimous oath?

There is some difference of opinion whether this clause should be enforced by national or by state authority; but surely that difference is not a very material one. If the slave is to be surrendered, it can be of but little consequence to him or to others by which authority it is done; and should any one, in any case, be content that this oath shall go unkept on a merely unsubstantial controversy as to how it shall be kept?

Again, in any law upon this subject, ought not all the safe-

guards of liberty known in civilized and humane jurispru-
dence to be introduced, so that a free man be not, in any case,
surrendered as a slave? And might it not be well at the same
time to provide by law for the enforcement of that clause in
the Constitution which guarantees that "the citizens of each
state shall be entitled to all the privileges and immunities of
citizens in the several states?"

I take the official oath to-day with no mental reservations,
and with no purpose to construe the Constitution or laws by
any hypercritical rules; and while I do not choose now to
specify particular acts of Congress as proper to be enforced, I
do suggest that it will be much safer for all, both in official
and private stations, to conform to and abide by all those acts
which stand unrepealed, than to violate any of them, trusting
to find impunity in having them held to be unconstitutional.

It is seventy-two years since the first inauguration of a
President under our National Constitution. During that
period, fifteen different and very distinguished citizens have in
succession administered the executive branch of the Government. They have conducted it through many perils, and generally with great success. Yet, with all this scope for precedent, I now enter upon the same task, for the brief constitutional term of four years, under great and peculiar difficulties.

A disruption of the Federal Union, heretofore only men-
aced, is now formidably attempted. I hold that in the contemplation of universal law and of the Constitution, the union
of these states is perpetual. Perpetuity is implied, if not expressed, in the fundamental law of all national governments.
It is safe to assert that no government proper ever had a provision in its organic law for its own termination. Continue to
execute all the express provisions of our National Constitution,
and the Union will endure forever, it being impossible to destroy it except by some action not provided for in the instrument itself.

Again, if the United States be not a government proper, but
an association of states in the nature of a contract merely, can
it, as a contract, be peaceably unmade by less than all the
parties who made it? One party to a contract may violate it

—break it, so to speak; but does it not require all to lawfully rescind it? Descending from these general principles, we find the proposition that in legal contemplation the Union is perpetual, confirmed by the history of the Union itself. The Union is much older than the Constitution. It was formed, in fact, by the Articles of Association in 1774. It was matured and continued in the Declaration of Independence in 1776. It was further matured, and the faith of all the then thirteen states expressly plighted and engaged that it should be perpetual, by the Articles of the Confederation, in 1778; and finally, in 1787, one of the declared objects for ordaining and establishing the Constitution was to form a more perfect Union. But if the destruction of the Union by one or by a part only of the states be lawfully possible, the Union is less perfect than before, the Constitution having lost the vital element of perpetuity.

It follows from these views that no state, upon its own mere motion, can lawfully get out of the Union; that resolves and ordinances to that effect are legally void; and that acts of violence within any state or states against the authority of the United States are insurrectionary or revolutionary, according to circumstances.

I therefore consider that, in view of the Constitution and the laws, the Union is unbroken, and, to the extent of my ability, I shall take care, as the Constitution itself expressly enjoins upon me, that the laws of the Union shall be faithfully executed in all the states. Doing this, which I deem to be only a simple duty on my part, I shall perfectly perform it, so far as is practicable, unless my rightful masters, the American people, shall withhold the requisition, or in some authoritative manner direct the contrary.

I trust this will not be regarded as a menace, but only as the declared purpose of the Union that it will constitutionally defend and maintain itself.

In doing this there need be no bloodshed or violence, and there shall be none unless it is forced upon the national authority.

The power confided to me *will be used to hold, occupy, and possess the property and places belonging to the Government,* and collect the duties and imposts ; but beyond what may be necessary for these objects there will be no invasion, no using of force against or among the people anywhere.

Where hostility to the United States shall be so great and so universal as to prevent competent resident citizens from holding federal offices, there will be no attempt to force obnoxious strangers among the people that object. While strict legal right may exist of the Government to enforce the exercises of these offices, the attempt to do so would be so irritating, and so nearly impracticable withal, that I deem it best to forego, for the time, the uses of such offices.

The mails, unless repelled, will continue to be furnished in all parts of the Union.

So far as possible, the people everywhere shall have that sense of perfect security which is most favorable to calm thought and reflection.

The course here indicated will be followed, unless current events and experience shall show a modification or change to be proper ; and in every case and exigency my best discretion will be exercised according to the circumstances actually existing, and with a view and hope of a peaceful solution of the national troubles, and the restoration of fraternal sympathies and affections.

That there are persons, in one section or another, who seek to destroy the Union at all events, and are glad of any pretext to do it, I will neither affirm nor deny. But if there be such, I need address no word to them.

To those, however, who really love the Union, may I not speak, before entering upon so grave a matter as the destruction of our national fabric, with all its benefits, its memories, and its hopes ? Would it not be well to ascertain why we do it ? Will you hazard so desperate a step, while any portion of the ills you fly from have no real existence ? Will you, while the certain ills you fly to are greater than all the real ones you fly from ? Will you risk the commission of so fearful a mistake ? All profess to be content in the Union if all constitutional rights can be maintained. Is it true, then, that any right, plainly written in the Constitution, has been denied ? I think not. Happily the human mind is so constituted that no party can reach to the audacity of doing this.

Think, if you can, of a single instance in which a plainly-written provision of the Constitution has ever been denied. If, by the mere force of numbers, a majority should deprive a minority of any clearly-written constitutional right, it might, in a moral point of view, justify revolution ; it certainly would if such right were a vital one. But such is not our case.

All the vital rights of minorities and of individuals are so plainly assured to them by affirmations and negations, guarantees and prohibitions in the Constitution, that controversies never arise concerning them. But no organic law can ever be framed with a provision specifically applicable to every question which may occur in practical administration. No foresight can anticipate, nor any document of reasonable length contain, express provisions for all possible questions. Shall fugitives from labor be surrendered by national or by state authorities ? The Constitution does not expressly say. Must Congress protect slavery in the Territories ? The Constitution does not expressly say. From questions of this class spring all our constitutional controversies, and we divide upon them into majorities and minorities.

If the minority will not acquiesce, the majority must, or the Government must cease. There is no alternative for continuing the Government but acquiescence on the one side or the other. If a minority in such a case will secede rather than acquiesce, they make a precedent which, in turn, will ruin and divide them, for a minority of their own will secede from them whenever a majority refuses to be controlled by such a minority. For instance, why not any portion of a new Confederacy, a year or two hence, arbitrarily secede again, precisely as portions of the present Union now claim to secede from it ? All who cherish disunion sentiments are now being educated to the exact temper of doing this. Is there such perfect identity of interests among the states to compose a new Union as to produce harmony only, and prevent renewed secession ? Plainly, the central idea of secession is the essence of anarchy.

A majority held in restraint by constitutional check and limitation, and always changing easily with deliberate changes of popular opinions and sentiments, is the only true sovereign of a free people. Whoever rejects it, does, of necessity, fly to anarchy or to despotism. Unanimity is impossible; the rule of a minority, as a permanent arrangement, is wholly inadmissible. So that, rejecting the majority principle, anarchy or despotism, in some form, is all that is left.

I do not forget the position assumed by some that constitutional questions are to be decided by the Supreme Court, nor do I deny that such decisions must be binding in any case upon the parties to a suit, as to the object of that suit, while they are also entitled to a very high respect and consideration in all parallel cases by all other departments of the Government ; and while it is obviously possible that such decision may be erroneous in any given case, still the evil effect following it, being limited to that particular case, with the chance that it may be overruled and never become a precedent for other cases, can better be borne than could the evils of a different practice.

At the same time the candid citizen must confess that if the policy of the Government upon the vital question affecting the whole people is to be irrevocably fixed by the decisions of the Supreme Court, the instant they are made, as in ordinary litigation between parties in personal actions, the people will have ceased to be their own masters, unless having to that extent practically resigned their Government into the hands of that eminent tribunal.

Nor is there in this view any assault upon the Court or the Judges. It is a duty from which they may not shrink, to decide cases properly brought before them ; and it is no fault of theirs if others seek to turn their decisions to political purposes. One section of our country believes slavery is right and ought to be extended, while the other believes it is wrong and ought not to extended ; and this is the only substantial dispute ; and the fugitive slave clause of the Constitution, and the law for the suppression of the foreign slave-trade, are each as well, enforced, perhaps, as any law can ever be in a community where the moral sense of the people imperfectly supports the law itself. The great body of the people abide by the dry legal obligation in both cases, and a few break over in each. This, I think, cannot be perfectly cured, and it would be worse in both cases after the separation of the sections than before. The foreign slave-trade, now imperfectly suppressed, would be ultimately revived, without restriction, in one section ; while fugitive slaves, now only partially surrendered, would not be surrendered at all by the other.

Physically speaking, we cannot separate; we cannot remove our respective sections from each other, nor build an impassable wall between them. A husband and wife may be divorced, and go out of the presence and beyond the reach of each other, but the different parts of our country cannot do this. They cannot but remain face to face ; and intercourse, either amicable or hostile, must continue between them. Is it possible, then, to make that intercourse more advantageous or more satisfactory after the separation than before ? Can aliens make treaties easier than friends can make laws ? Can treaties be more faithfully enforced between aliens than laws can among friends ? Suppose you go to war, you cannot fight always ; and when, after much loss on both sides and no gain on either, you cease fighting, the identical questions as to terms of intercourse are again upon you.

This country, with its institutions, belongs to the people who inhabit it. Whenever they shall grow weary of the existing government, they can exercise their constitutional right of amending, or their revolutionary right to dismember or overthrow it. I cannot be ignorant of the fact that many worthy and patriotic citizens are desirous of having the National Constitution amended. While I make no recommendation of amendment, I fully recognize the full authority of the people over the whole subject, to be exercised in either of the modes prescribed in the instrument itself, and I should, under existing circumstances, favor, rather than oppose, a fair opportunity being afforded the people to act upon it.

I will venture to add that to me the convention mode seems preferable, in that it allows amendments to originate with the people themselves, instead of only permit'ing them to take or reject propositions originated by others not especially chosen for the purpose, and which might not be precisely such as they would wish either to accept or refuse. I understand that a proposed amendment to the Constitution (which amendment, however, I have not seen) has passed Congress, to the effect that the Federal Government shall never interfere with the domestic institutions of states, including that of persons held to service. To avoid misconstruction of what I have said, I depart from my purpose not to speak of particular amendments, so far as to say that, holding such a provision to now be implied constitutional law, I have no objection to its being made express and irrevocable.

The Chief Magistrate derives all his authority from the people, and they have conferred none upon him to fix the terms for the separation of the states. The people themselves, also, can do this if they choose, but the Executive, as such, has nothing to do with it. His duty is to administer the present government as it came to his hands, and to transmit it unimpaired by him to his successor. Why should there not be a patient confidence in the ultimate justice of the people? Is there any better or equal hope in the world? In our present differences is either party without faith of being in the right? If the Almighty Ruler of nations, with his eternal truth and justice, be on your side of the North, or on yours of the South, that truth and that justice will surely prevail by the judgment of this great tribunal, the American people. By the frame of the Government under which we live, this same people have wisely given their public servants but little power for mischief, and have with equal wisdom provided for the return of that little to their own hands at very short intervals. While the people retain their virtue and vigilance, no administration, by any extreme wickedness or folly, can very seriously injure the Government in the short space of four years.

My countrymen, one and all, think calmly and well upon

this whole subject. Nothing valuable can be lost by taking time.

If there be an object to hurry any of you, in hot haste, to a step which you would never take deliberately, that object will be frustrated by taking time ; but no good object can be frustrated by it.

Such of you as are now dissatisfied still have the old Constitution unimpaired, and on the sensitive point, the laws of your own framing under it ; while the new administration will have no immediate power, if it would, to change either.

If it were admitted that you who are dissatisfied hold the right side in the dispute, there is still no single reason for precipitate action. Intelligence, patriotism, Christianity, and a firm reliance on Him who has never yet forsaken this favored land, are still competent to adjust, in the best way, all our present difficulties.

In your hands, my dissatisfied fellow-countrymen, and not in mine, is the momentous issue of civil war. The Government will not assail you.

You can have no conflict without being yourselves the aggressors. You have no oath registered in heaven to destroy the Government, while I shall have the most solemn one to " preserve, protect, and defend" it.

I am loth to close. We are not enemies, but friends. We must not be enemies. Though passion may have strained, it must not break, our bonds of affection.

The mystic cords of memory, stretching from every battle-field and patriot grave to every living heart and hearthstone all over this broad land, will yet swell the chorus of the Union, when again touched, as surely they will be, by the better angels of our nature.

THE EMANCIPATION PROCLAMA-TION.

The Civil War and Slavery.

DURING the earlier period of the Civil War it was very generally hoped that some settlement of the questions at issue might be reached without any prolonged contest. But as the conflict deepened and gradually assumed vaster proportions, the conviction gained ground that neither party would yield until their resources were exhausted.

Almost at the outset of the war, not a few active and influential individuals had urged that the most effective means of bringing the South to terms was the emancipation of the slaves. Such a policy, however, was not favorably entertained by the majority of the people at the North. At the same time it was thoroughly understood that slavery was the real cause of the conflict, and that permanent peace would thereafter be impossible unless measures were adopted for its abolition.

On March 6, 1862, Mr. Lincoln sent a message to Congress, recommending that the United States should grant pecuniary aid to such States as would agree "to adopt a gradual abolition of slavery." Such a measure was accordingly introduced, and after some vehement opposition was adopted by both Houses of Congress, and approved by the President, April 10th. A Bill providing for emancipation in the District of Columbia was also passed, a few days later.

The primary object of Mr. Lincoln in the conduct of the war had been the restoration of the Union. When criticised by some of the more ardent advocates of emancipation, he replied, in his usual forceful way: " My paramount object is to save the Union, and not either to save or destroy slavery. If I could save the Union without freeing any slave, I would do it ; if I could save it by freeing all the slaves, I would do it ; and if I could do it by freeing some and leaving others alone, I would also do that." In this, as in all other important matters, it was a part of his policy not to anticipate public sentiment but to act in harmony with it. As an evidence of a growing sentiment favorable to emancipation, representative men from both the East and the West as well as deputations from several religious bodies sought interviews with him respecting this subject.

Satisfied, at length, that he had the constitutional authority to take the step, and that it would receive the moral support of the great body of the people, he issued, on the 22d of September, a Preliminary Emancipation Proclamation. In this document he declared his purpose, on the first day of January, 1863, to issue a Proclamation announcing that "all persons held as slaves within any State, or designated part of a State, the people whereof shall then be in rebellion against the United States, shall be then, thenceforward, and forever free."

This Proclamation provoked a variety of criticism, but, on the whole, received the approval of the loyal people of the North. It served to define more clearly the issue between parties, and strengthened the loyalty of the army.

In the fulfillment of his declared purpose, President Lincoln issued, January 1, 1863, the Emancipation Proclamation. This paper is almost entirely ministerial in its tone and contents, enumerating the several States or parts of States in which emancipation should take effect, and ordering the army and navy to protect the persons thus restored to freedom. One paragraph— that in which an appeal is made " to the considerate judgment of mankind, and to the gracious favor of Almighty God "—is conspicuous for its dignity and beauty, and this was written by Secretary Chase, the President inserting the words "upon military necessity." Mr. Lincoln always regarded this as the central act of his administration, and the great act of the nineteenth century.

The results both immediate and remote of the Emancipation Proclamation have been very clearly presented by Mr. Holland in his *Life of President Lincoln.* He says: " This document involved the liberty of four millions of human beings then living, and of untold millions then unborn ; it changed the policy and the course and character of the war, revolutionized the social institutions of more than a third of the nation, and brought all the governments of Christendom into new relations to the rebellion."

With admirable insight Mr. Boutwell (in *Rice's Reminiscences of President Lincoln*) has characterized Mr. Lincoln's peculiar merit as the author of the Proclamation. He says : "There is no other individual act performed by any person on this continent that can be compared with it. The Declaration of Independence and the Constitution were each the work of bodies of men. The Proclamation of Emancipation in this respect stands alone. The responsibility rests wholly upon Lincoln ; the glory is chiefly his. No one can now say whether the Declaration of Independence, the Constitution, or the Proclamation of Emancipation was the highest, best gift to the country and to mankind."

PROCLAMATION OF EMANCIPATION.

January 1, 1863.

Whereas, on the twenty-second day of September, in the year of our Lord one thousand eight hundred and sixty-two, a proclamation was issued by the President of the United States, containing, among other things, the following, to-wit :

" That on the first day of January, in the year of our Lord one thousand eight hundred and sixty-three, all persons held as slaves within any state or designated part of a state, the people whereof shall then be in rebellion against the United States, shall be then, thenceforward, and forever free ; and the Executive Government of the United States, including the military and naval authority thereof, will recognize and maintain the freedom of such persons, and will do no act or acts to repress such persons or any of them, in any efforts they may make for their actual freedom.

" That the Executive will, on the first day of January aforesaid, by proclamation, designate the states and parts of states, if any, in which the people thereof respectively shall then be in rebellion against the United States ; and the fact that any state, or the people thereof, shall on that day be in good faith represented in the Congress of the United States, by members chosen thereto at elections wherein a majority of the qualified voters of such state shall have participated, shall, in the absence of strong countervailing testimony, be deemed conclusive evidence that such state, and the people thereof, are not then in rebellion against the United States."

Now, therefore, I, ABRAHAM LINCOLN, President of the United States, by virtue of the power in me vested as Commander-in-Chief of the army and navy of the United States in time of actual armed rebellion against the authority and government of the United States, and as a fit and necessary war measure for suppressing said rebellion, do, on this first day of January, in the year of our Lord one thousand eight hundred and sixty-three, and in accordance with my purpose so to do, publicly proclaimed for the full period of one hundred days from the day first above mentioned, order and designate, as the states and parts of states wherein the people thereof respectively are this day in rebellion against the United States, the following, to-wit:

Arkansas, Texas, Louisiana (except the parishes of St. Bernard, Plaquemine, Jefferson, St. John, St. Charles, St. James, Ascension, Assumption, Terre Bonne, Lafourche, St. Marie, St. Martin, and Orleans, including the city of New Orleans), Mississippi, Alabama, Florida, Georgia, South Carolina, North Carolina, and Virginia (except the forty-eight counties designated as West Virginia, and also the counties of Berkely, Accomac, Northampton, Elizabeth City, York, Princess Anne, and Norfolk, including the cities of Norfolk and Portsmouth), and which excepted parts are for the present left precisely as if this proclamation were not issued.

And, by virtue of the power and for the purpose aforesaid, I do order and declare that all persons held as slaves within said designated states and parts of states are and henceforth shall be free; and that the Executive Government of the United States, including the military and naval authorities thereof, will recognize and maintain the freedom of said persons.

And I hereby enjoin upon the people so declared to be free, to abstain from all violence, unless in necessary self-defense ; and I recommend to them that in all cases, when allowed, they labor faithfully for reasonable wages.

And I further declare and make known that such persons

of suitable condition will be received into the armed service of
the United States, to garrison forts, positions, stations, and
other places, and to man vessels of all sorts in said service.

And upon this act, sincerely believed to be an act of justice,
warranted by the Constitution, upon military necessity, I
invoke the considerate judgment of mankind and the gracious
favor of Almighty God.

In testimony whereof, I have hereunto set my name, and
caused the seal of the United States to be affixed.

Done at the city of Washington, this first day of January, in
the year of our Lord one thousand eight hundred and
[L.S.] sixty-three, and of the Independence of the United
States the eighty-seventh.

                                        ABRAHAM LINCOLN.

By the President :
WILLIAM H. SEWARD, *Secretary of State.*

THE GETTYSBURG ADDRESS.

THE battle of Gettysburg marks the turning point of the Civil War. It was fought on the 1st, 2d, and 3d of July, 1863; and resulted in the defeat of the invading troops under Gen. Lee and in the abandonment of the invasion of Pennsylvania. The contest was one of the most sanguinary of the whole war, the losses in the Union army amounting to more than twenty-three thousand. With a spirit of commendable liberality and patriotism the State of Pennsylvania purchased seventeen and a half acres of land, forming an important part of the battlefield, to be used as a national burying-ground. On November 19th, 1863, this cemetery was formally dedicated with impressive ceremonies in the presence of the President and the members of his Cabinet. A large and imposing military display added to the impressiveness of the occasion. Mr. Edward Everett delivered a formal oration, but President Lincoln made the brief address which will forever be known in American literature as the Gettysburg Address. It was not written until after he left Washington, and in the intervals of such leisure as he could command before reaching the cemetery.

These twenty lines are full of the spirit of true eloquence. A great occasion prompted a great man to utter a few words that will forever find a response in all loyal, patriotic souls. The religious earnestness with which, on this recent battle-field, Mr. Lincoln dedicates himself to the unfinished task still before him, reveals the heart of one profoundly moved by the occasion, and inspired by a lofty, moral purpose. It is sufficient to add that these sentiments are uttered in simple and forceful words, happily suited to the thought. The public reading of this Address on stated occasions by the pupils of our schools would be an exercise admirably adapted to foster sentiments of the purest patriotism.

Mr. George Boutwell, as quoted in *Rice's Reminiscences of Mr. Lincoln*, puts the following estimate upon this Address:

"This oration ranks with the noblest productions of antiquity, with the works of Pericles, of Demosthenes, of Cicero, and of the finest passages of Grattan, Burke, or Webster. This is not the opinion of Americans only, but of the cultivated in other countries whose judgment anticipates the judgment of posterity."

Another competent writer thus anticipates the verdict of posterity :

"That literature is immortal which commands a permanent place in the schools of a country, and is there any composition more certain of that destiny than Lincoln's Oration at Gettysburg?"

SPEECH AT THE DEDICATION OF THE NATIONAL CEMETERY AT GETTYSBURG.

November 15, 1863.

Fourscore and seven years ago our fathers brought forth upon this continent a new nation, conceived in liberty, and dedicated to the proposition that all men are created equal. Now we are engaged in a great civil war, testing whether that nation, or any nation so conceived and so dedicated, can long endure. We are met on a great battle-field of that war. We have come to dedicate a portion of that field as a final resting-place for those who here gave their lives that that nation might live. It is altogether fitting and proper that we should do this. But in a larger sense we cannot dedicate, we cannot consecrate, we cannot hallow this ground. The brave men, living and dead, who struggled here, have consecrated it far above our power to add or detract. The world will little note, nor long remember, what we say here ; but it can never forget what they did here. It is for us, the living, rather to be dedicated here to the unfinished work which they who fought here have thus far so nobly advanced. It is rather for us to be here dedicated to the great task remaining before us, that from these honored dead we take increased devotion to that cause for which they gave the last full measure of devotion ; that we here highly resolve that these dead shall not have died in vain ; that this nation, under God, shall have a new birth of freedom, and that government of the people, by the people, and for the people, shall not perish from the earth.

www.ingramcontent.com/pod-product-compliance
Lightning Source LLC
Chambersburg PA
CBHW031750090426
42739CB00008B/950